Why Should I Hire You?

How to Do Well in Job Interviews

by

J. Michael Farr
&
Susan Christophersen

Why Should I Hire You?

How to do Well in Interviews
© 1992 by JIST Works, Inc.

Published by JIST Works, Inc.
720 North Park Avenue
Indianapolis, IN 46202-3490
Phone: 317-264-3720 Fax: 317-264-3709 E-Mail: jist works@aol.com
World Wide Web Address: http://www.jist.com

Other Books in the *Living Skills* Series:

- *The Two Best Ways to Find a Job*
- *The Skills Advantage*
- *An Introduction to Job Applications*
- *Effective Communications Skills*
- *You Can Bank on It!*
- *Checking and Savings Accounts*
- *Consumer Loans & Credit Cards*

JIST publishes and distributes hundreds of other career-related books, videos, software, assessment devices, and other materials. Please contact the publisher or your distributor for additional details.

Cover Design by Dean Johnson Design Group

Printed in the United States of America.

99 98   9 8 7 6 5

We have been careful to provide accurate information throughout this book, but it is possible that errors and omissions have been introduced. Please consider this in making any career plans or other important decisions. Trust your own judgment above all else and in all things.

ISBN 1-56370-039-5

Table of Contents

CHAPTER ONE

What Is an Interview?

The goals of this chapter are:

- ✪ *To understand the purpose of an interview.*
- ✪ *To begin thinking about the good-worker traits employers look for.*

Don't Wait for the Job to Open

People usually think of an interview as a meeting with an employer when there is a job opening. You find out about a job opening, and you call to set up an interview.

But you don't have to wait until you hear about a job opening. You can get an interview even if an employer doesn't have a job opening now.

Read the story that follows. It will show you why it's good to get interviews whether there is a job opening or not. Then answer the questions that follow the story.

Making a Good Impression Pays Off Later

Kim Taylor is a restaurant manager. She is sitting in her office working at her desk. Someone knocks on her door. Assistant manager Mark Hoffman enters.

Mark: *(Looking worried)* I came to tell you that Bill Jones in the kitchen just quit. Do you want me to put an ad in the want ads tomorrow? We can't afford to be understaffed in the kitchen.

Kim: No, hold off on the ad. Someone came in here a few weeks ago. . . let's see, what was her name? Mullins? No, Marilyn. That's it. Marilyn Gilbert.

Mark: Marilyn Gilbert? I remember her.

Kim: *(She opens a drawer in her desk and pulls out a file folder.)* I wrote her name down and put it in a file. I was really impressed with her. Let's give her a call and see if she's still looking for work. I've got a few other people in mind, too, if she's not available.

Mark: That's great. It will save us a lot of time and trouble if we don't have to advertise.

Kim: *(Smiling)* That's the idea.

The job seeker, Marilyn Gilbert, knew there were no job openings when she came in. But Marilyn asked for an interview anyway. She hoped to make a positive impression on the manager in case a job opened up. Marilyn did make a good impression. As a result, Marilyn was the first person the manager thought of to replace a worker who was leaving.

➤ Think About It

1. Why did the assistant manager, Mark Hoffman, seem worried when an employee gave his notice to leave?

   _____

   _____

   _____

2. Why did Kim Taylor, the manager, think of Marilyn Gilbert when she found out there was a job to be filled?

   _____

   _____

   _____

3. Why would both managers be pleased about hiring Marilyn, rather than advertising the job opening?

   _____

   _____

   _____

Notes

✪ Write down any questions you have about what you have just read or make notes about things you want to remember.

   _____

   _____

   _____

   _____

   _____

   _____

   _____

   _____

Employers Like to Save Time and Money

Employers like to save money on advertising. They also like to make the hiring process as smooth as possible. You can save employers time and money if you present yourself as a possible worker now or for the future.

LEARNING KEY

An interview is a chance to talk with someone who hires people with skills like yours.

Don't wait for a job opening. Go talk to employers *before* the job opens up. Then they might hire you instead of advertising a job that opens up later. That can happen *if* you make a good impression. This book shows you how to make a good impression in your job interviews. It will also help you get the job you want.

➤Challenge

You are the owner of a small business. Your success depends on the kinds of workers you employ to keep the business running smoothly. You decide to post a notice on an employee bulletin board. The notice lists the ''good worker'' traits that you value most.

What traits are on your list?

✪ Write these traits in the notice below.

Hint: *Think about what it takes for people to work together to accomplish a goal or a task.*

NOTICE TO EMPLOYEES

Please Observe the Following Requirements:

Good-Worker Traits

Good-worker traits are the skills that make you a good worker. All employers look for people with these skills. Some examples of good-worker traits are getting to work every day on time, honesty, getting the job done, getting along with co-workers and working hard. Often, employers won't hire a person who does not have or use these skills.

CHAPTER TWO

Know What You Want in a Job and What You Can Do

The goals of this chapter are:

- ✪ *To understand why you need to know your skills and your job objective.*
- ✪ *To make sure that you can state your job objective clearly.*

Be Prepared to Show an Employer What You Have to Offer

Most people work because they have to. But it is also possible to like your job and the work you do. The key is to know your best skills. These are skills you do well and enjoy using.

Know Your Skills

The story that follows shows the importance of knowing what your skills are and what you have to offer an employer.

Vanessa sat on the top step of her front porch. She tossed pebbles, one by one, down onto the sidewalk. She looked sad. Her Uncle Pete drove up and parked beside the curb. He got out of the car and walked over to Vanessa.

Uncle Pete: *What's the matter?*

Vanessa: *Mom won't let me take the car. I need a job so I can buy my own car.*

Uncle Pete: *What kind of job do you want?*

Vanessa: *I don't know. Whatever's out there.*

Uncle Pete: *So you'll just go out and say, "Hey, will you please hire me because I'm a nice person and I need to buy a car?"*

Vanessa: *Well, everybody works because they need money.*

Uncle Pete: *That may be one reason people work, but it's not the reason people get hired.*

Vanessa: *It's not?*

Uncle Pete: *Employers really don't care if you want to buy a car. They want to know what you have to offer. What can you do? What makes you a good worker?*

Vanessa: *I haven't thought about that.*

Uncle Pete: *Well, get yourself a pen and paper. Then write down your ideas about what you can do for an employer. Your next step is to find employers who might need someone like you. Later on you can work on what they can do for you.*

Vanessa: *Do you know anyone who could hire me, Uncle Pete?*

Uncle Pete: *(Smiling) That depends on what you can do. Write down some ideas. Then I might be able to give you a few leads.*

➤ What Are Your Skills?

1. In the spaces that follow, write down the kinds of jobs you might look for.

   _____

   _____

   _____

2. Write down the three things about yourself that make you a good worker. For example, you might be dependable, hard working, or able to get along with others.

   a. _____

   b. _____

   c. _____

3. Make a list of the skills you have that qualify you for these jobs. What do you have to offer the employer?

   _____   _____

   _____   _____

   _____   _____

   _____   _____

   _____   _____

   _____   _____

   Hint: The list you just made is your ticket to getting the job you want! If you know your skills and can talk about them with confidence, you are well on your way to having successful interviews.

Notes

✪ Write down questions you have about what you have just read or make notes about things you want to remember.

   _____

   _____

   _____

   _____

   _____

   _____

   _____

   _____

Know Your Job Objective

Your ability to talk about your skills will help you do well in your job interviews. You also need to have a clear job objective. You need to know what you want, or it might not be what you get.

The conversation between two friends that follows will show why you need to have a clear job objective.

Gina: *Hi, Tony. Long time no see. What have you been doing lately?*

Tony: *Trying to find a job. I haven't had any luck yet.*

Gina: *(Laughing) What's luck got to do with it?*

Tony: *Oh, you know. Being in the right place at the right time and all that.*

Gina: *What kind of job are you looking for?*

Tony: *I'm not really too picky. I'll take what I can get.*

Gina: *Well, what do you want in a job? Do you want to work for a big company or a small one? Do you want to work indoors or out? What sorts of things do you want to do? What are you good at? Do you like to sit still, or move around a lot? What kind of pay do you need, and how many hours can you work?*

Tony: *Good grief! I don't know. I haven't thought about all that stuff.*

Gina: *You know, Tony, I think you'd have an easier time finding a job if you could tell people what kind of work you're looking for. I found that out myself, when I was looking for a job.*

Tony: *But I can do a lot of different things. I don't want to box myself in to one or two things. It seems like that would make it harder to find a job.*

Gina: *Employers don't want to hire people who say they'll do just anything. They want people who know what they can do, and what they want to do. Once I figured out what I really wanted, and what I could do, things started happening. I found more opportunities, not less!*

Tony: *Well, I can see your point, and it makes sense. I guess I'll go home and figure out what I really want. Thanks, Gina.*

➤Think About It

✪ Before you go any further in this book, be sure you know what your job objective is. Answer the questions that follow to see whether you do. Check Yes or No in the box beside each question.

JOB OBJECTIVE FACTORS	YES	NO
I know what kind of work I want to do.		
I know what skills I need to do this work.		
I know what kind of work matches my training and/or experience.		
I know the work environment I like to work in (indoor, outdoor, noisy, quiet, busy, slow, etc.).		
I know what wages or salary I need to earn, and what this kind of work pays.		

Hint: If you answered "No" to any of the questions, your job objective is not yet clear enough. You will need to spend more time to figure out the sort of job you want and the skills you need to do it. Do this before you begin your job search.

➤Challenge

You are listening to your favorite radio station. A contest has just been announced. If you are the ninth caller, you will win a prize. The prize is the job you've always wanted. But you have to describe the job and the skills you have to do it in only 30 seconds.

You dial the telephone number. Sure enough, you are the ninth caller. You win! The disc jockey asks you to describe the job you want and the skills you have. The second hand on the clock is ticking away. You have 30 seconds. What will you say?

Hint: You have more than 30 seconds to complete this exercise. When you are done, you should be able to make a clear, brief statement about what you want and what you can do.

✪ Describe your "dream" job below and the skills you have to do it.

_____

_____

_____

_____

_____

_____

_____

_____

_____

Know Your Skills Language

Now that your job objective is clear, and you know your skills and the type of job you want, you can practice what you will say at an interview. It is very important to develop a "skills language." You need to be able to tell an employer what you can do before an employer will hire you.

Notes

✪ Write down questions you have about what you have just read or make notes about things you want to remember.

_____

_____

_____

_____

_____

_____

_____

_____

CHAPTER THREE

What an Employer Expects

The goals of this chapter are:

- ✪ *To understand what an employer expects of you.*
- ✪ *To learn how to meet those expectations.*

An Employer Wants Solid Evidence

When you go to an interview, you meet with someone who gathers information about you. An interviewer is like a private detective. He or she looks for evidence that shows whether you are the right person for the job. To find the evidence, an interviewer looks for certain clues. If an interviewer finds the evidence he or she is looking for, you might be hired. If the interviewer doesn't find the right evidence, you will be screened out.

Many people feel nervous about going to interviews. But if you know how to give the right impression or "evidence," you can go to an interview with more confidence.

Here are three kinds of clues or indicators an employer looks for:

1. Do you present yourself well?
2. Are you reliable?
3. Can you do the job?

CLUE #1: *Do you present yourself well?*

Many people feel that it's not fair to judge people by their appearance. Fair or not, it happens anyway. How you look and how you act tells an interviewer a lot about your self-respect. How you present yourself also shows how much you pay attention to detail.

Dress and Grooming

What you wear to an interview depends on what kind of job you are applying for. There is no standard uniform that works for every job interview. An office worker would not wear the same kind of clothing as a construction worker. The best rule to follow for what to wear on an interview is this:

LEARNING KEY

Dress as you think your supervisor would dress—but neater.

If you are not sure how the supervisor would dress, ask around. Ask parents, friends, teachers, and others. Avoid clothes that are either too casual or too dressy for the job. Remember, you want to make the very best impression possible.

Pay attention to details of appearance and personal hygiene. Such details include:

- ✪ Neat hairstyle
- ✪ Fingernails clean and trimmed
- ✪ Shoes shined
- ✪ Clothes clean, pressed and conservative (not trendy)

- ✪ Make-up not too heavy
- ✪ Handshake and Eye Contact
- ✪ No perfume or cologne (or very light)

Job seekers are often told to offer the interviewer a firm handshake at the start and end of the interview. They are also told to make plenty of eye contact.

Do what makes you feel comfortable. A handshake is a good idea if you can do it with confidence. Looking directly into someone's eyes can make you feel more nervous, if you aren't used to doing that.

Try practicing these things with a friend or family member before you try them in an interview. Practice shaking hands in case the interviewer offers it. Practice will make you feel more confident.

Posture and Personal Habits

Posture is another way to give positive clues about yourself. If you sit in an interview, sit up straight or lean forward a little. Look interested.

Try to keep your hands still. Don't gesture a lot, or use nervous habits. Smile when you get the chance, and don't chew gum. Also, don't smoke, even if the interviewer asks if you want to.

CLUE #2: *Are you reliable?*

During the interview, look for chances to tell the interviewer how reliable you are. Those chances will come in the questions the interviewer asks. You will learn more about how to answer interview questions in chapter 4.

An employer is really trying to find out if you:

✪ Show up for work on time   ✪ Get along well with other employees

✪ Get things done on time   ✪ Can be trusted

LEARNING KEY

One way to show an employer that you are reliable is to be on time for the interview.

CLUE #3: *Can you do the job?*

An employer will look for clues that prove you have the skills, training, or experience to handle the job. For entry level jobs, you might not need experience or training. But you must show that you can learn to do the job.

LEARNING KEY

If you give the right clues in an interview, you stand a good chance of getting the job.

Again, the questions you are asked during the interview will be your chance to show that you have the skills to learn the job.

The story that follows is about the second interview between Kim Taylor, the restaurant manager, and Marilyn Gilbert, the job seeker. Mrs. Taylor called Marilyn to see if she still wanted the job. They arranged another interview.

Selling Yourself—"Clinching the Deal"

During her previous interview with Mrs. Taylor, Marilyn had noticed that the manager wore slacks and a blouse on the job. Marilyn followed the rule about dressing like the supervisor. For this interview, she wore dress slacks and a nice blouse. Her shoes matched her slacks.

Mrs. Taylor and Marilyn are talking in Mrs. Taylor's office. Marilyn answers Mrs. Taylor's questions carefully. Notice how she finds ways to talk about her skills.

Mrs. Taylor:	*Hello, Miss Gilbert. I'm glad you could meet with me today. Won't you sit down?*
Marilyn:	*Thank you. I'm glad to be here too.*
Mrs. Taylor:	*Although we spoke a few weeks ago, I'd like to ask you a few more questions. Why are you interested in this job?*
Marilyn:	*This job would require me to use my best skills, which are cooking and working under pressure. I like the challenge of working fast but still doing the job right. I know that in a restaurant customers want their food fast. And they want it to taste good.*
Mrs. Taylor:	*It sounds as though you have worked for a restaurant before. What is your experience?*
Marilyn:	*I don't have actual experience in a restaurant, but I am the oldest of five children. My mother has worked full-time for years, and I've often been in charge of making the meals for my brothers and sisters. Keeping everybody happy and well-fed has been one of my main responsibilities at home. And of course, they like to bring their friends over sometimes too! Our relatives in the area come over for big Sunday dinners, so I've cooked for a crowd many times.*
Mrs. Taylor:	*Have you ever had any other kind of training for this work?*
Marilyn:	*I have taken classes in school related to cooking, and last year I attended a day-long seminar that was put on by a local catering company. It was about catering for special parties and events, and planning the stages of a meal. We learned some special recipes and cooking tips, too.*
Mrs. Taylor:	*You mentioned that cooking at home for your brothers and sisters was one of your main responsibilities. What would happen if your work hours conflicted with your work at home?*
Marilyn:	*Of course I take my responsibilities at home seriously. But I never make an outside commitment unless I have worked out ways to keep that commitment. My mother and I have discussed this thoroughly. We have made arrangements for the children when I work. Also, they are getting old enough now to take more care of themselves.*

After a few more questions, Mrs. Taylor offered Marilyn the job. Then they talked about Marilyn's wages and work hours.

➤Challenge

Imagine the following situation. You have just interviewed for a job. The person who interviewed you sends a memo about you to other people in the company who will be deciding who to hire for the job.

✪ What would you want the memo to say about you? Write the memo in the space below from the point of view of the person who interviewed you.

Hint: Remember the three kinds of clues an employer looks for. Comments on these clues are likely to be the main part of the memo.

MEMORANDUM

TO:

FROM:

REASON:

DATE:

➤ Think About It

1. What are some ways to give an interviewer positive clues about yourself?

   _____

   _____

   _____

2. Do you have an "interview outfit" or two ready? What will you wear?

   _____

   _____

   _____

3. In her interview with Mrs. Taylor, Marilyn gave examples to support her skills. Name some examples Marilyn used to support her skills.

   _____

   _____

   _____

Notes

✪ Write down questions you have about what you have just read or make notes about things you want to remember.

   _____

   _____

   _____

   _____

   _____

   _____

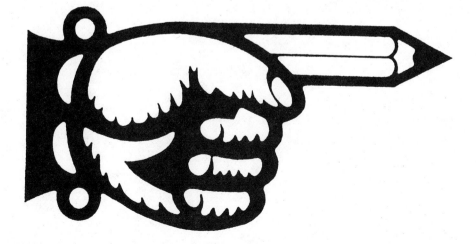

CHAPTER FOUR

Giving the Right Clues:
The 3-Step Process for
Answering Interview Questions

The goals of this chapter are:

- ✪ *To learn a process to handle any interview question you might be asked.*
- ✪ *To practice answering the most common (and hardest) interview questions.*

Handling Interview Questions

The most important part of the interview is how you answer questions. No book can tell you exactly what questions you will be asked. But you can learn how to handle most questions that comes your way.

LEARNING KEY

The best way to answer interview questions is to understand what clues the employer is looking for, and what clues you need to give.

We have said that an interviewer is like a detective looking for clues. Remember, the interviewer is watching for these clues you give about yourself:

✪ Do you present yourself well?   ✪ Can you do the job?

✪ Are you reliable?

An interview is also a test of your communications skills. Communicating involves listening and talking. The process you learn about in this chapter shows you how to listen and talk effectively during an interview.

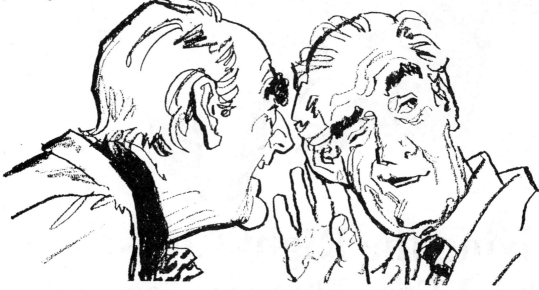

The 3-Step Process for Answering Interview Questions

Below are the three steps you can use in answering most interview questions. Following the steps is a sample interview question and how the 3-Step Process can be used to answer it.

✪ **STEP 1:** *Understand what is really being asked.*

✪ **STEP 2:** *Present the facts to make yourself look good.*

✪ **STEP 3:** *Give examples to support your best skills.*

SAMPLE INTERVIEW QUESTION: *How will you get to work if you take this job?*

STEP 1: *Understand what is really being asked.*

If you don't think about what the interviewer is really asking, you might answer, "I'll drive my car," or "I'll take the bus," or "My Aunt Nancy will give me a lift." But the interviewer doesn't really care how you will get to work. What the interviewer does care about is whether you have reliable transportation so that you can be on time to work everyday. In other words, the question is, "Are you reliable?" Now that you know what clue the interviewer is looking for, move on to Step 2.

STEP 2: *Present the facts to make yourself look good.*

You can use each interview question to bring out something positive about yourself. Go back to the sample question, "How will you get to work?" You could say, "I don't have a car, but I live two blocks from the bus line. The bus always runs and I never have to worry about my car not starting on cold mornings!" With that answer, you have told the interviewer not to worry. You have a reliable way to get to work on time. Besides answering the interviewer's real concern, you can make your answer even better. Step 3 shows you how.

STEP 3: *Give examples to support your skills.*

You might not realize it, but the ability to be on time for an appointment or for work is a skill. It's one thing to say, "I'm always on time." But you will make a bigger impression on the interviewer if you can give an example.

Go back to the sample question, "How will you get to work?" You could say, "I've always made a habit of being on time when I have made a commitment. When I was in school, I was always on time for my classes."

Good Listening Helps You Give Good Answers

The question, How will you get to work?" seemed simple enough. But with the 3-Step Process you just learned, you can make a question like that work for you. Here is the entire answer you could give. See how much more this answer accomplishes than simply saying, *"I'll take the bus?"*

> *"I don't have a car, but I live just two blocks from the bus line. I've been using the bus for a long time, and I never have to worry about my car not starting on cold mornings! And of course, I've always made it a habit to be on time when I make a commitment. When I was in school, I was always on time for my classes."*

➤ Practicing the 3-Step Process for Answering Interview Questions

✪ Practice answering interview questions using the 3-Step Process. You need practice because you won't have 10 minutes to think about every answer during the interview. Once you get the hang of it, your answers will come more quickly to you. Take as much time as you need to think about each part of each question. Each of the following questions are ones that job seekers find hard to answer. They are also often asked in interviews.

SAMPLE QUESTION #1: *Why should I hire you?*

> *Hint: This is THE most important question for you to answer well in the interview!*

STEP 1: *What is really being asked?*

_____

_____

_____

_____

STEP 2: *How can you use this question to make yourself look good?*

_____

_____

_____

_____

STEP 3: *What are some examples you can give to support your skills?*

> *Hint: Use this question as a chance to point out your very best skills.*

_____

_____

_____

_____

✪ Now write your answer to Sample Question #1:

_____

_____

_____

_____

_____

_____

_____

SAMPLE QUESTION #2: *Can you tell me a little about yourself?*

STEP 1: *What is really being asked?*

_____

_____

_____

_____

STEP 2: *How can you use this question to make yourself look good?*

_____

_____

_____

_____

STEP 3: *What are some examples you can give to support your skills?*

> *Hint: Use this question to talk about your accomplishments such as good grades, past job experience, or other successes.*

_____

_____

_____

_____

✪ Now write your answer to Sample Question #2:

_____

_____

_____

_____

_____

_____

_____

_____

_____

SAMPLE QUESTION #3: *Why do you want this job?*

> **STEP 1:** *What is really being asked?*

_____

_____

_____

_____

> **STEP 2:** *How can you use this question to make yourself look good?*

_____

_____

_____

_____

> **STEP 3:** *What are some examples you can give to support your skills?*
>
> **Hint:** *Use this question to explain what you have to offer the business or organization. Don't talk about what you want the company to give you.*

_____

_____

_____

_____

✪ Now write your answer to Sample Question #3:

_____

_____

_____

_____

_____

_____

_____

SAMPLE QUESTION #4: *What kind of training or experience do you have for this job?*

STEP 1: *What is really being asked?*

_____

_____

_____

_____

STEP 2: *How can you use this question to make yourself look good?*

_____

_____

_____

_____

STEP 3: *What are some examples you can give to support your skills?*

> *Hint: If you have training or experience, don't be modest! If you don't, then let the interviewer know that you are eager and willing to learn.*

_____

_____

_____

_____

✪ Now write your answer to Sample Question #4:

_____

_____

_____

_____

_____

_____

_____

SAMPLE QUESTION #5: *What are your strongest skills for this job?*

STEP 1: *What is really being asked?*

_____

_____

_____

_____

STEP 2: *How can you use this question to make yourself look good?*

_____

_____

_____

_____

STEP 3: *What are some examples you can give to support your skills?*

> ***Hint:*** *The interviewer is giving you a chance to give strong clues about your good worker traits. Again, don't be modest!*

_____

_____

_____

_____

✪ Your Answer to Sample Question #5:

_____

_____

_____

_____

_____

_____

_____

SAMPLE QUESTION #6: *What areas are you weak in?*

STEP 1: *What is really being asked?*

_____

_____

_____

_____

STEP 2: *How can you use this question to make yourself look good?*

_____

_____

_____

_____

STEP 3: *What are some examples you can give to support your skills?*

> ***Hint:*** *Everyone has at least some weaknesses. A good response to this kind of question would be to talk about how you plan to improve.*

_____

_____

_____

_____

✪ Now write your answer to Sample Question #6:

_____

_____

_____

_____

_____

_____

_____

SAMPLE QUESTION #7: *What sorts of problems have you had in previous jobs?*

STEP 1: *What is really being asked?*

_____

_____

_____

_____

STEP 2: *How can you use this question to make yourself look good?*

_____

_____

_____

_____

STEP 3: *What are some examples you can give to support your skills?*

> *Hint: The ability to learn from mistakes or problems is an excellent skill. Use this question to show that you have a positive attitude toward solving problems. Don't put former employers or co-workers down.*

_____

_____

_____

_____

✪ Now write your answer to Sample Question #7:

_____

_____

_____

_____

_____

_____

_____

_____

SAMPLE QUESTION #8: *If we hired you, how would you help make our organization better?*

STEP 1: *What is really being asked?*

_____

_____

_____

_____

STEP 2: *How can you use this question to make yourself look good?*

_____

_____

_____

_____

STEP 3: *What are some examples you can give to support your skills?*

       Hint: This is another chance to show what you have to offer the employer.

_____

_____

_____

_____

✪ Now write your answer to Sample Question #8:

_____

_____

_____

_____

_____

_____

_____

SAMPLE QUESTION #9: *If you could design a job for you that would be perfect, what would that be?*

STEP 1: *What is really being asked?*

_____

_____

_____

_____

STEP 2: *How can you use this question to make yourself look good?*

_____

_____

_____

_____

STEP 3: *What are some examples you can give to support your skills?*

> *Hint: This is not the time to talk about your fantasy of becoming a famous rock star. Use this question to talk about how important it is to you to use your best skills in the work you do. Skills that, of course, you would be using in the job you are applying for.*

_____

_____

_____

_____

✪ Now write your answer to Sample Question #9:

_____

_____

_____

_____

_____

_____

_____

_____

SAMPLE QUESTION #10: *How well do you handle responsibility?*

STEP 1: *What is really being asked?*

_____

_____

_____

_____

STEP 2: *How can you use this question to make yourself look good?*

_____

_____

_____

_____

STEP 3: *What are some examples you can give to support your skills?*

Hint: Describe ways you have handled responsibility in the past, and ways you have improved. You might say, "I do best when I take on more responsibility gradually, as I adjust to the job." This tells the interviewer that you won't take on more than you can handle. It also tells the interviewer that you are eager to improve.

_____

_____

_____

_____

✪ Now write your answer to Sample Question #10:

_____

_____

_____

_____

_____

_____

_____

_____

SAMPLE QUESTION #11: *What do you like to do in your spare time?*

    STEP 1: *What is really being asked?*

_____

_____

_____

_____

    STEP 2: *How can you use this question to make yourself look good?*

_____

_____

_____

_____

    STEP 3: *What are some examples you can give to support your skills?*

        Hint: *You don't have to (and shouldn't) give the interviewer a list of all the things you do when you are goofing off. Talk about one or two activities that show interests or skills related to the job you want.*

_____

_____

_____

_____

✪ Now write your answer to Sample Question #11:

_____

_____

_____

_____

_____

_____

_____

_____

The Question of Pay

There is one question that the 3-Step Process does not work well with. This is the question about what you want to be paid for the job you will do.

Find out before the interview what wages are typical for this job. Also, have a good idea what you need to earn. You should look for a job that will allow you to meet all your expenses.

The interviewer may ask, "What do you expect to be paid?" Try to avoid answering this question until you are offered the job. There are two reasons to avoid the question. First, you might expect too much. Then the employer will feel that you won't be satisfied with a lower wage. Second, you might name a lower wage than the employer planned to pay. Then you get the job, but you lose the better wage.

A good way to avoid answering the question, "What do you expect to be paid?" is to ask a question in return. Such as, "What does this position pay?" Many employers will tell you.

However, some will insist that you answer the question. In that case, give a salary range that most similar jobs would pay. For example you might give one of the ranges below.

RANGE OF PAY
$5 to $8 an hour, or $7 to $10 an hour
$200 to $300 per week, or $300 to $400 per week

By giving a big range of pay, you are less likely to be eliminated because you are asking too much or too little. Base your answer on what you think is fair and reasonable.

What If You Can't Answer an Interview Question?

Don't panic. If you are feeling very nervous, take a deep breath and count to 10. Concentrate on what the interviewer is saying. The problem might be that you simply did not understand the question. If that happens, you can say, "I'm sorry, but I'm not sure I understand the question. Could you please say it another way?" Then listen very carefully, use the 3-Step Process, and do the best you can.

➤Challenge

✪ Imagine that you are in an interview. The interviewer is going to ask you only one question. (In reality, this is very unlikely. But this is a question you MUST be prepared to answer, in one form or another.) The question is, *"Why should I hire you?"* What will you say? Write your answer below.

_____

_____

_____

_____

_____

_____

_____

_____

_____

_____

_____

_____

_____

➤ Think About It

1. What key skills are involved in answering interview questions?

   _____

   _____

   _____

   _____

   _____

2. How much do you need to make on your next job to be able to meet your expenses?

   _____

   _____

   _____

   _____

   _____

3. Review the interview question worksheets you completed. Are there any questions you still don't feel comfortable answering? Practice them now until you feel confident.

   _____

   _____

   _____

   _____

   _____

Notes

✪ Write down questions you have about what you have just read or make notes about things you want to remember.

   _____

   _____

   _____

   _____

   _____

   _____

   _____

   _____

CHAPTER FIVE

Building Confidence for Your Interviews

The goals of this chapter are:

- ✪ *To feel confident in how you talk about yourself.*
- ✪ *To learn how you can ask questions in the interview.*
- ✪ *To learn what to do after an interview.*

An Interview Is No Time to Be Modest

It should be clear by now that an interview is no time to be modest! Even if it feels like bragging, practice talking about your best points. Remember to support them with examples.

Employers won't hire you because you seem "nice." They will hire you if they believe you can do the job. How else can they know that if you don't tell them?

Talk About Your Best Points and Speak with Self-Confidence

Employers look for people who can do the job. Even if you believe you can do the job, you must convince the employer to hire you. Having confidence in yourself will help you tell an employer about your skills for the job.

➤ Challenge

✪ Let's do an exercise about speaking with confidence. First, read the list of statements that follow. Put a check mark on the line beside each statement that sounds like something you might say. Next, in the spaces following each statement, write a better version of the statement. Change each statement as much as you feel is necessary. Remember, you want to give the interviewer positive clues about yourself.

1. "I'm okay with my hands, I guess."

_____

_____

2. "I'm pretty good about getting places on time, most of the time."

_____

_____

3. "I don't really have any actual experience, but I'm pretty sure I can learn."

_____

_____

4. "I thought that maybe you'd have some kind of job for a person like me."

_____

_____

5. "I know I'm probably not as qualified as a lot of other people, but I really hope you'll give me a chance anyway."

_____

_____

6. "I guess I want this job because your ad sounded like something I might be able to do."

_____

_____

7. "Reliable? Yeah, I'm pretty reliable. I mean, it's not like I'd be calling in sick all the time, or anything like that."

_____

_____

Tips for Speaking with Confidence

Here are some tips you can use to be more aware of how you speak about yourself.

- ✪ **DON'T** put yourself down with negative statements like: "I know I'm probably not as qualified as a lot of other people..."

- ✪ **DON'T** use weak words such as "pretty good," "I guess," "might be able to," "I thought that maybe..." Don't apologize for your lack of experience. Instead, point to any life experience or training you can use to support your good worker traits.

- ✪ **DO** use words that show you have faith in yourself. For example: "I am very good with my hands;" "I am always on time;" "I believe your organization would benefit from having a person with my skills..."

- ✪ **DO** answer the interviewer's real concern. Say positive things about yourself. For example: "Yes, I am reliable. I know how important it is to show up for work every day and do the job right."

Making Positive Statements

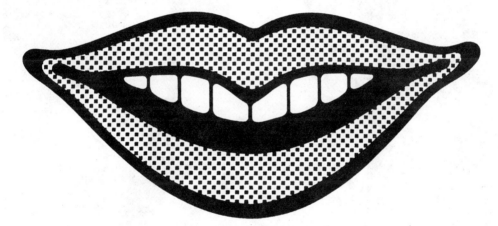

These statements that follow are similar to the ones you read in the previous exercise. Can you see the difference? The earlier statements belong to a person with low self-confidence. This set of statements, however, shows strength and self-esteem. If you were an employer, which type of person would you want to hire?

1. "One of my best skills is working with my hands."
2. "I always try to be on time, whatever the situation."
3. "I have had many experiences that needed the kind of skills I would use on this job. Let me give you some examples...."
4. "I'd like to talk with you about the skills I have to offer your organization."
5. "I believe I have the skills needed to handle this job, and I'd be happy to have the chance to show you that."
6. "When I saw your advertisement, I knew I had the skills you were looking for."
7. "Yes, I consider myself a very reliable person. Let me give you some examples...."

Speaking with self-confidence takes practice. You can practice every day, starting now. Notice how you talk about yourself in ordinary conversation. Most of us are not aware of our negative speech habits. Get used to using the language of self-confidence every day. Then you will not feel awkward when you use it in your interviews.

You Can Ask Questions, Too

It's a good idea to find out about an organization before you interview for a job there. You can do this by talking to people who work there. You may be able to get some information from the library. Or you can call the receptionist and ask some brief questions. But you might not be able to learn much about the job until you are actually **in** the interview. This section will show you how you can get information during an interview.

EXAMPLE: *Asking Questions*

Read what follows. Notice how the job applicant found ways to ask questions about the organization.

Interviewer:	*This job requires someone who can work fast and efficiently. Can you work under pressure?*
Applicant:	*I actually work better under pressure. I like the challenge. How big of a volume do you do here on an average day?*
Interviewer:	*We have a lot of different people who work here each day. Do you usually get along well with other employees you work with?*
Applicant:	*I think people work best together when they are willing to cooperate and help each other out. How many employees do you have here?*

You and the interviewer can both gather the kind of information you need to decide whether you are right for the job, and the job is right for you.

Closing the Interview

There are two things you should do at the end of an interview. If you want the job, the first thing to do is to say so. The second thing is to arrange for a time to call the employer back. You will call to find out if a decision has been made about hiring you. This is called the Call Back Close.

EXAMPLE: *A Call Back Close*

Read what follows. It shows you what we mean by a Call Back Close. This dialogue takes place at the end of an interview.

Interviewer: *(Rising from her chair) Well, thank you very much for coming in, Miss Stevens. It's been nice talking with you.*

Applicant: *I've enjoyed meeting you, too, Miss Stevens. I want you to know that I am interested in this job. It is just what I have been looking for and I would be willing to work hard to show you that I could do it. When could I call you if I have any questions? (or, When do you think you will make a decision?)*

Make sure you get a day and time to call back. Then put that date on your calendar and call on time.

After the Interview—Follow Up!

After the interview, plan to follow up. The first thing to do is to send a thank-you note. Then schedule follow up phone calls. Remember the story about Marilyn Gilbert? In her case, the employer called her when a job opened. But you don't have to wait, hoping for a call. Your chance of being hired is better if you take control and call the employer. You should wait a few days, but not too long.

If you sent a thank-you note right after the interview, they will remember that when you call back. If you want the job, say so when you call the employer. If the employer has not yet made a decision, call back again in another few days or so.

LEARNING KEY
Following up after the interview is almost as important as the interview itself.

If you interviewed before there was a job opening, call back from time to time to let the employer know you are still interested. The idea is to keep in touch, and to make sure they don't forget you.

Thank-You Notes

Sending a thank-you note after an interview is one of the things that will give you an edge over other job seekers. A thank-you note is a courtesy that creates a very positive impression. It also helps employers remember your name.

Here is an example of a thank-you note. Marilyn Gilbert sent this note to Mrs. Taylor, the restaurant manager, after their first interview.

November 30, 19XX

Dear Mrs. Taylor,

I want to thank you for taking the time to meet with me recently. I was very impressed with your company and the state-of-the-art equipment your facility utilizes. I am very interested in this type of work and would be willing to work hard if you had a job opening in the future. I look forward to meeting with you again.

Sincerely,

Marilyn Gilbert

Marilyn Gilbert

Tips for Writing Thank-You Notes

- ✪ Use nice stationery with a simple "Thank You" on the front. You can buy this at a stationery store. Beige, light gray, or off-white colors are best.
- ✪ Write it out by hand (unless your handwriting is hard to read).
- ✪ Address the interviewer formally (Dear Mr. Brown, Dear Ms. Smith). Don't use first names.
- ✪ Keep the note short.
- ✪ Send the note right after the interview.

If you are wondering whether a thank-you note is worth the effort, remember Marilyn Gilbert. The manager of the restaurant said she had "a few other people in mind" for the job. But it was Marilyn's name she thought of first. Marilyn's thank-you note made a difference.

➤ Challenge

✪ Write a newspaper feature article about your first interview (you will have to imagine it). Use as much of the information you have learned in this book as you can for your article. Write about the interview from beginning to end. Include getting ready, the interview itself, and follow-up. To get started, read the following first few lines of the sample article below.

Kurt Wannaget, age 21, got up on Wednesday morning, took a shower, and ate his Wheaties (Breakfast of Champions). He dressed for his interview in dark blue slacks, black shoes (recently shined) and a white shirt. Carrying a notebook containing information he might need for his application, Wannaget made sure he got to the bus stop early for the trip downtown. He arrived at Company WSB several minutes early and reported to the receptionist.

✪ Now, continue this exercise by writing about **your** interview below. Use your own paper if you run out of space.

_____

_____

_____

_____

_____

_____

_____

_____

_____

_____

_____

_____

_____

➤ Think About It

1. What are some ways you can improve on how you talk about yourself?

   _____

   _____

   _____

   _____

2. How can you find out information about organizations that have jobs you might want?

   _____

   _____

   _____

   _____

3. What is the value of a thank-you note after an interview?

   _____

   _____

   _____

   _____

Notes

✪ Write down questions you have about what you have just read or make notes about things you want to remember.

   _____

   _____

   _____

   _____

   _____

   _____

   _____

   _____

WRITE IT DOWN!

CHAPTER SIX

Interview Readiness

The goals of this chapter are:

- ✪ *To find out how ready you are for your first interview.*
- ✪ *To use role-playing to practice for your interviews.*

Are You Ready?

You have learned most of the basics you need in order to do well in your interviews. This chapter provides interview checklists, practice techniques, and a few final pointers to help you do well in your interviews.

The following Readiness Checklist will help you get organized before the interview and help prepare you to make a good impression during an interview.

➤ Readiness Checklist

✪ Imagine that you have an interview later today. Get ready for everything, including showering, getting dressed, gathering any information you need to take with you, and so on. Then use the checklist that follows to see what you thought to do and what you overlooked.

DID YOU REMEMBER TO	
_____ Plan your transportation to the interview?	_____ Keep from drinking too much coffee (to keep from being jittery)?
_____ Find out what kind of pay is typical for this job?	_____ Find out what you could about the organization?
_____ Eat a good meal?	_____ Arrange child care if necessary?

Gather information you might need to fill out an application (references' names and telephone numbers, former employers' names and addresses, school addresses and dates of completion, etc.).

ARE YOUR	DO YOU FEEL
_____ Clothes clean, pressed, and attractive?	_____ Confident and relaxed (as much as possible)?
_____ Shoes shined?	_____ Alert and focused?
_____ Make-up, jewelry, and cologne understated?	_____ Ready to answer questions (using the 3-Step Process)?
	_____ Sure of what you can do to make a good impression? (Remember the three kinds of clues an employer looks for.)

LEARNING KEY
The more confident you feel, the better you will do in your interviews.

Hint: Go over these checklists again when you are getting ready for your real interviews.

➤Challenge

This next exercise is best done with someone else. If a friend, relative or someone else is not available, then you can practice by yourself. You are going to practice for an interview by role playing. You will pretend that you are in a real interview.

- ✪ You will be the job applicant. You will answer questions similar to those you practiced in chapter 4. If you do this with another person, switch roles after you practice as applicant. This will help each of you get a feel for how the interviewer observes a job applicant.

- ✪ To make this exercise more effective, use the space below to write down some notes about the kind of job you plan to look for. Give these notes to the person who is role-playing as your "interviewer." Include ideas about what type of organization it is, what your duties would be, how many hours a week it would be, and other details. If possible, come to the role play dressed as you plan to dress for your interviews.

➤Think About It

1. Go back to the start of each chapter in this book. Review the goals of each chapter. Decide for yourself whether you have reached the stated goals. What can you do to make sure you reach all the goals?

_____

_____

_____

_____

2. Spend the time you need to work on any area of interviewing that you do not understand or do not feel comfortable with. What can you do to improve?

_____

_____

_____

_____

3. If you're not sure about what to wear, ask someone you know and respect to help you pick out your clothes for the interview. List the clothes and accessories you will wear below.

_____

_____

_____

_____

4. Are you comfortable shaking hands with someone you don't know? If not, practice until it becomes easier. What else can you do to appear confident and self-assured?

_____

_____

_____

_____

Notes

✪ Write down questions you have about what you have just read or make notes about things you want to remember.

_____

_____

_____

_____

_____

_____

➤Role Play

Part I—The Beginning

✪ An interview often starts with a few moments of light conversation. This is the "warm-up" time. With your partner, spend a few minutes saying hello, shaking hands, settling into your seats and remarking on the weather (or whatever). It is often helpful to make a positive comment on the organization or on something you see in the interviewer's office.

Part II—The Middle

You and the interviewer have become acquainted. Now it's time for the serious business of the interview to take place. Remember the 3-Step Process when you answer questions.

THE 3-STEP PROCESS
1. Understanding what is really being asked.
2. Present the facts to make yourself look good.
3. Give examples to support your skills.

✪ The questions below ask the same kinds of questions you reviewed in chapter 4. They are not exactly the same, because every interviewer is different. If you have trouble answering these questions, you can refer back to chapter 4. Make a note of the questions you found hard to answer. Practice these questions until you feel that you can handle them. Try to use the 3-Step Process to answer each one.

1. Tell me about your abilities to do this job.

_____

_____

_____

2. Tell me about your background.

_____

_____

_____

3. Why are you applying for this job?

_____

_____

_____

4. How do I know you can do the job?

_____

_____

_____

5. What are your best skills?

_____

_____

_____

6. What are your weaknesses (or strengths) for this job?

_____

_____

_____

7. What benefits do you need to be happy with a job?
   Hint: This could mean salary, insurance benefits, vacation, etc.

_____

_____

_____

8. Have you ever been fired or had problems in past jobs?

_____

_____

_____

9. What can you offer this organization?

_____

_____

_____

10. What is your ideal job?

_____

_____

_____

11. Do you like a lot of responsibility?

_____

_____

_____

12. Why should I hire you? (This is the most important question of all!)

_____

_____

_____

The "interviewer" can add more questions. You can ask the interviewer questions about the job. The more "real" you can make this practice interview, the more prepared you will be for your actual interviews.

Part III—The End

The interview is coming to an end. The interviewer will probably thank you for coming in. Remember to:

- ✪ Thank the interviewer for taking the time to meet with you.
- ✪ Ask for the job. (If you want it.)
- ✪ Ask when a good time would be to call back.

Hint: If you do want the job, you can get this across by saying something like, "I know I could do a good job for you, and I'd really like the chance to show you that."

Part IV—Follow-Up

Write a brief thank-you note to your interviewer. (Make sure you have found out how to spell his or her name. When you do this after a real interview, call the receptionist or someone at the company if you're not sure how to spell the name.)

Imagine that it is a few days after the interview you role-played. Make a telephone call to your interviewer. Tell them why you want the job and why you think you could do it well.

Parting Words

Congratulations! By completing this book, you have become a better job seeker. You are more likely to get the job you want than someone else who is less skillful in interviews.

Being well-prepared for job interviews can give you an edge over people who are just as qualified as you. If those people have not practiced interview skills, you can make a better impression.

Don't Get Discouraged

A job search is hard work. Give yourself the credit you deserve for making the effort to do that work well. But don't be discouraged if you don't get a job offer each time you have an interview. Being turned down as a job applicant does not affect your value as a person. Being turned down means that, for whatever reason, you were not considered the best person for the job. If that's true, then that job was not right for you.

You may go to many interviews before you find the job that's right. You can learn from each one of those interviews. Meanwhile, keep your spirits up, and do the best you can. That's the most that anyone can do, and that's enough.

Good luck!

Notes

Notes